PRIOR PARK
LANDSCAPE GARDEN

Bath

The National Trust

Prior Park Landscape Garden

A noble seat which sees all Bath and which was built for all Bath to see.

Philip Thicknesse, 1788

The beauty and interest of Prior Park Landscape Garden lies in its dramatic site, running down the small steep valley from the mansion to the Palladian Bridge and the very edge of Bath, the most fashionable spa of 18th-century England. It was created during the lifetime of one man, the entrepreneur and philanthropist Ralph Allen, from about 1734 until his death in 1764. With his architect John Wood the Elder and the master of ceremonies 'Beau' Nash, Allen transformed the old market town into the splendid Palladian city. Over 30 years he continuously landscaped, planted and gardened at Prior Park in three distinct phases (see pp.4–7). Although the 28-acre (11.3-hectare) landscape is now decayed, it has survived largely unchanged since his death.

Ralph Allen and Bath stone

Ralph Allen (1693–1764) came to Bath from Cornwall in 1710 and made his first fortune from reorganising the postal system. He began buying land in 1726, and his second fortune sprang from the stone quarries on Combe Down that built the new city. In 1724–5 he pioneered the Avon navigation scheme, which enabled Bath stone to be

Ralph Allen; by Thomas Hudson, c.1740 (Hurd Episcopal Library, Hartlebury). Alexander Pope called him 'the most noble man of England', praising his quiet philanthropy:

> Let humble ALLEN, with an aukward Shame,
> Do good by stealth, and blush to find it Fame.

shipped to Bristol and London. The Bristol engineer John Padmore built the crane at Allen's stone wharf depicted in the Bucks' c.1734 engraving of Bath, which also shows the end of the railway he constructed to transport the huge blocks of stone from the Combe Down quarries down to the river.

This radical method of haulage using gravity and rails considerably reduced the cost of Bath stone, but was not enough to win Allen the contract for part of Greenwich Hospital in 1728. The setback stimulated him to build his severe Palladian mansion on the superb site above the city to demonstrate the beauty and quality of his stone.

John Wood

The son of a Bath builder, Wood (1704–54) was imbued with the new Palladian style of architecture that Colen Campbell had demonstrated at Wanstead (1717) and Stourhead (1720). In 1727 he was engaged by Allen to enlarge his town house in Bath, still to be partly glimpsed in Lilliput Alley. A year later they were planning the mansion at Prior Park where work was under way by about 1734; Wood described the site: 'natural terraces rising above one another, like the stages between the seats of a Roman theatre'. Allen and Wood fell out in the late 1730s and after the latter's dismissal the construction of the east office wing and the house above basement level was supervised by Allen's clerk of works, Richard Jones, not to Wood's original design or approval. Allen moved in in 1741.

'The Man of Bath'

Allen was a self-made and benevolent man, who helped to found the Mineral Water Hospital in 1742 and endowed many other charities in Bath. At his new mansion, he entertained a creative circle of friends who included the Bath MP William Pitt the Elder, as well as writers like Alexander Pope, Samuel Richardson and Henry Fielding. Allen appears as Squire Allworthy in Fielding's *Tom Jones*:

> Neither Mr Allworthy's house nor his heart were shut against any part of mankind, but they were both more particularly open to men of merit. To say the truth, this was the only house in the kingdom where you were sure to gain a dinner by deserving it.

The stone wharf on the Avon, showing Padmore's crane and Allen's railway; detail from the Bucks' view of Bath c.1734

The view from South Parade in 1759, showing the stone wharf by the river and Prior Park on the skyline; pen and wash drawing by Thomas Robins

The development of the garden

Phase I (c.1734–44): Alexander Pope

Allen began planting around 1734. Anthony Walker's engraving of 1752 shows the garden below the house in the first phase, when it extended only halfway down the valley, terminating at the round pond and bounded by a low wall which permitted views out into the 'borrowed landscape' beyond. On the left (east) side, a straight hedge punctuated with urns on plinths indicates a formal layout and screens the vegetable garden and the pine house, which later became a cold bath (now vanished). By contrast, the right-hand (west) side of the lawn shows the Wilderness with a serpentine path. Within this area there are still the remains of irregular rococo features, strongly influenced and probably laid out by Allen's friend, the poet Alexander Pope.

Pope was a pioneer of the landscape movement with his *Guardian* essay (1713) and his *Epistle to Lord Burlington* (1731): 'In all, let Nature never be forgot ... Consult the Genius of the Place'. His own garden in the new freer English style was begun at Twickenham in 1720. Pope visited Bath in 1734 and corresponded with Allen, who visited him at Twickenham in 1736. He first came to Prior Park in 1737, making five more long visits – for three months in 1739 – before he died in 1744. He ordered Bath stone urns for his garden and recommended Lord Burlington's gardener, Henry Scot, to help Isaac Dodsley, Allen's head gardener, to grow pineapples. If Scot visited Prior Park, he would have encouraged here the latest more informal style of garden being undertaken at Chiswick at the same time by the landscape designer William Kent.

Thomas Thorpe's 1742 map of *The Country Round Bath* shows how conveniently Prior Park was sited on the route of Allen's railway between the Combe Down quarries and his wharf on the Avon. It also records the planting of formal avenues of trees south of the new house

(*Above*) The poet Alexander Pope, who stayed frequently at Prior Park in the 1740s; attributed to J.B. Van Loo (1 Royal Crescent, Bath)

(*Left*) Prior Park in 1752; engraving by Anthony Walker. Curious visitors look over the wall into the informal Wilderness, which contrasts with the more regular planting to the left of the central lawn. The railway on the right brought blocks of Bath stone from the Combe Down quarries to Prior Park and the riverside wharf at the bottom of the valley

The general formal shape of the grounds in the first phase, with straight edges to the planted areas either side of the lawn leading down only as far as the pond, and with formal avenues above the house, is indicated on Thorpe's 1742 map of *The Country Round Bath*. The irregular features in the Wilderness on the west side include a grotto, serpentine lake and sham bridge, described in more detail on pp.8–11.

Phase II (1744–c.1760): The Palladian Bridge

After Pope's death in 1744, Allen received plenty of advice from amateurs and friends, such as Sanderson Miller, who probably designed the Sham Castle further round the hillside, visible from his town house but not from Prior Park. Samuel Richardson described the scene in 1748:

> Below the House, the gardens were laid out on two terraces and two slopes; but all these are adorned with vases, ornaments and other Stonework; and the affluence of water is so great that it is received in three places; and after many agreeable falls, at the head of one is a statue of Moses [now gone], down to his knees, in an attitude expressive of the admiration he must have shown after striking the rock and seeing the water gush out of it.

The park was extended in the 1750s down to the bottom of the valley where the old fish ponds were enlarged. The Palladian Bridge was built here in 1755 by Richard Jones, who had taken over from John Wood. The bridge was the third such structure to be built in England and is described in more detail on p.14. A large cascade flanked by thick planting was constructed on the slope below the Round Pond at the old boundary of the garden, as can be seen in a drawing of about 1758 by the Bath artist Thomas Robins. At much the same time the woodland fringes were made more informal according to the characteristic English landscape style. Most of the original trees have gone, but many were replanted in the 19th century. Notable recent losses have been all the elms (through Dutch elm disease) and a strategically placed old oak in the park half-way down the valley.

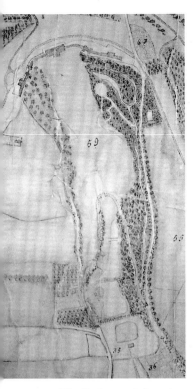

The final, more informal landscape created by 'Capability' Brown is shown on Thorpe and Overton's c.1762 Survey

(*Opposite*) Thomas Robins's c.1758 pen and wash sketch shows the central cascade which initially interrupted the view from the Palladian Bridge up towards the house. A series of dams created further smaller waterfalls below the bridge

'Capability' Brown, who opened up the landscape in the early 1760s; portrait by Nathaniel Dance (National Portrait Gallery)

Phase III (c.1760–4): 'Capability' Brown

Allen employed the landscape designer 'Capability' Brown to carry out the third and last phase of the garden in the early 1760s. It seems to have been Brown who took away the divisive central cascade and united the whole valley in one great sweep of parkland between the Palladian master-pieces of the house and the bridge. At the same time he reinforced and informalised the structural planting either side.

Since then, very little change has taken place in this picturesque scene. Thorpe and Overton's survey plan of Prior Park c.1762 records this final Brownian layout, but also shows that Allen retained features of the first phase in the Wilderness, where they did not intrude upon the larger scene.

Tour of the garden

The Wilderness

Mrs Allen's Grotto

The visitor enters the garden by the Middle Gate on Ralph Allen Drive, through the gate piers of the new drive made below the house in the 1830s. Before turning off the drive past the ticket kiosk on the left, follow the carriageway for 50 yards to find, beside a spring on the right-hand side, the ruins of Mrs Allen's Grotto. This was an elaborate feature dating from the 1740s encrusted with rare minerals sent from Cornwall,

(*Above*) The father of the Allens' dog Miss Bounce appears in William Kent's sketch of Pope's garden at Twickenham

(*Right*) Pope in his grotto at Twickenham; sketch by William Kent, *c.*1725–30 (Chatsworth). In its final form, his grotto was built from Bath stone given by Allen and lined with rare Cornish minerals supplied by William Borlase, who described it as:

> A natural cave in which the passenger may even entertain himselfe with all the delicacies of subterraneous nature, and more justifiably delay his entrance for a while into the Elyzium it leads him to.

like Pope's famous grotto at Twickenham. The floor survives and is made of pebbles, bones and ammonites, 'arranged in tasteful forms' of sunrays. Ralph Allen's wife Elizabeth received much encouragement from Pope, who wrote in August 1740 to 'rejoice extraordinarily that Mrs Allen has begun to imitate the Great Works of Nature, rather than those Baubles most Ladies affect'. Within the Grotto is buried Miss Bounce, a Great Dane puppy given to the Allens by the poet in 1739. The epitaph, inscribed on a stone slab in the floor, read:

> Weep not,
> Tread lightly my grave,
> Call me Pet.

Miss Bounce was one of a number of puppies given by Pope to the owners of the early landscape parks at Chiswick, Stowe and Cirencester. The carriage drive of 1830 unfortunately cuts off the Grotto from the rest of the Wilderness, but originally the water flowed on down by a statue of Moses into the Serpentine Lake. Return to the ticket kiosk and descend by the path to the site of the Serpentine Lake (now filled in).

Mrs Allen's grotto was lined with Cornish minerals like these illustrated in William Borlase's *Natural History of Cornwall* (1758), to which Ralph Allen subscribed

(*Left*) This sketch of Alexander Pope is said to have been made at Prior Park without him knowing by William Hoare (National Portrait Gallery)

The Serpentine Lake

This remarkable feature proved to be somewhat overambitious, as recent excavations by the Bath Archaeological Trust have revealed. The first thin, long lake on the side of the hill had straight stone edges but these were soon afterwards replaced by a serpentine stone retaining wall that ran along the contour as far as the Sham Bridge. However, this proved unable to hold back the long sheet of water and collapsed. The lake was filled in at a later date and replaced at the far end, near the bridge, by a round pond. The possibility exists to dig out and restore the Serpentine Lake, the main feature of the Wilderness.

The Cascade and the Cabinet

The path continues along the lower edge of the Serpentine Lake and crosses the rocky Cascade fed by springs above. The water below the Cascade continues in runnels and culverts by an open area about 25 metres wide known as the Cabinet.

Only some old yews remain of the original planting, remnants of a mixture of trees, shrubs and evergreens that would have divided the discrete elements of the Wilderness. No record of Pope's planting here exists, but the style of the time was to use a dense matrix of mixed shrubs and evergreens planted regularly in rows. These would have quickly coalesced to form an intimate mixture. The bank between the drive and the site of the Serpentine Lake has been planted in this manner with shrubs, including Portuguese laurel, *Philadelphus coronarius*, *Daphne laureola*, *Viburnum tinus* and butcher's broom, as well as yew, cherry and box elder.

Beyond, where the Wilderness meets the park, are the foundations of the Gothic Temple, added about 1754. This fell into ruin and was removed and rebuilt on a neighbouring property in 1921.

The Sham Bridge

Continuing to the far end of the Serpentine Lake, the later round pond lies before the Sham Bridge. This, with its vermiculated stone and three pediments, is the best surviving feature of Pope's work in the Wilderness, and was designed to look like a bridge over a river as one approached. The illusion of the bridge depends upon it being framed by evergreens, and so yews have been planted on the bank behind to replace common laurels introduced comparatively recently. There are also some False Acacias (*Robinia pseudoacacia*) here which could be progeny of an original tree.

The Sham Bridge on Thorpe and Overton's *Survey* of *c.*1762

The Sham Bridge in 1979

A woodcut of the Gothic Temple, *c.*1800

The park

Emerging from the Wilderness, the visitor follows the grazing fence separating the parkland from the school property. From here is the familiar view down the valley to the fish ponds and the Palladian Bridge, with Widcombe church and Bath beyond. There is no evidence that a permanent park fence existed in the 18th century, but the restored iron rail is traditional and necessary for grazing purposes. Behind stands the massive mansion, whose original severity is tempered by the splendidly curving steps added in 1834 for Bishop Baines, who had purchased Prior Park in 1829 for a Roman Catholic seminary and boys' college. The great house has survived two terrible fires, in 1836 and again in 1991, and the school completed its admirable restoration in 1995.

The walk down to the lakes

The path continues to the left, down the eastern side of the valley within the woodland, passing the site of the cold bath where there is a fine Oriental Plane (*Platanus orientalis*), apparently the sole survivor of a group of three original trees. Further down, where a little stream tumbles down the bank, there are the remains of an early

20th-century flower garden, an extension to the garden of the Priory above (built as the head gardener's cottage and now belonging to the school). Above the path may be discovered a timber structure of this period, which gives shelter from the rain. There are contrasting areas of dark evergreens and mature beech, and open areas with views over the parkland and, lower down, to the bridge, emerging at the bottom of the valley.

Fishponds Cottage lies on the right, and beyond it was the site of the original Priory house of Prior Park, the country estate of the Prior of Bath Abbey. There is a choice of crossing the fish ponds by the nearer dam, or the lower dam, from which the romantic view back up the valley reflects the house in the water. The banks of the enlarged ponds were evidently intended to remain evenly sloped, clear of vegetation and irregular only where this can be perceived from the house. On the bank above is the site of a circular ice-house, where ice for the kitchen was stored before the era of mechanical refrigeration.

(*Left*) This sketch by Thomas Robins from below the Palladian Bridge shows the Gothic Temple under the trees in the background

(*Centre*) The view from the mansion down to the Palladian Bridge in 1900

(*Below*) The Palladian Bridge from the park, with Widcombe Manor and church beyond; pen and wash drawing by Thomas Robins, 1758

The Palladian Bridge

The Prior Park bridge appears in the background of Gainsborough's 1766 portrait of the great actor David Garrick, who sought Allen's advice when he was thinking of buying a house in Bath in 1756. The Allens shared Garrick's veneration of Shakespeare: the eight-volume edition published in 1747 by their mutual friend Bishop Warburton is dedicated to Elizabeth Allen

(*Right*) The Palladian Bridge at Stowe

(*Opposite*) The Palladian Bridge

This type of covered bridge originates with that built by Andrea Palladio (1508–80) over the River Brenta at Bassano in northern Italy, which was constructed of wood and roofed to keep off the Alpine snow. Palladio also designed an architecturally elaborate bridge with covered shops for the Rialto in Venice, but it was not built, the present bridge over the Grand Canal owing more to Palladio's follower, Vincenzo Scamozzi.

The 9th Earl of Pembroke and his architect Roger Morris designed the first Palladian Bridge in England at Wilton in 1737. The Palladian Bridge at Stowe was completed the following year. The Prior Park bridge was built by Richard Jones in 1755 and differs from these in that the central columns of the loggia are wider apart than the others. Standing on the bridge one can appreciate the fine classical detailing of Allen's Bath stone.

In England in the 18th century there were two other similar structures, probably of wood, at Hagley, Worcestershire (1764), and Dogmersfield, Hampshire. Thomas Pitt, 1st Lord Camelford designed the Hagley bridge; he was the nephew of Allen's friend William Pitt and has been proposed as the designer at Prior Park. The other splendid marble bridge of similar design is at Tsarskoe Selo (1771) outside St Petersburg.

The bridge stands on the first of the three dams which forms a cascade through the central arch. As well as being seen as a bridge over apparently continuous water, it was framed by hanging woods. After clearance of overgrown laurel these banks have been replanted with yew, ash and lime instead of elm, which succumbs to disease. Alder and wild cherry have also been planted as quick-growing nurses, and mixed shrubberies are being introduced here and on the lower dam.

The walk back up to the entrance

Leaving the bridge the path turns up the west side of the valley and then to the right by the track that was made to bring the stone for the bridge from the quarries at Combe Down. Leaving the site of the ice-house and an octagonal thatched building below on the right, this track turns sharply again at the Rock Gate on Ralph Allen Drive. The gate belongs to the second phase of the garden, c.1755, when the fashion for Chinese and rustic garden ornaments of this kind had been established in England about 20 years.

The path then turns south along the boundary up the west side of the valley with views out across it and regains the ticket kiosk and entrance gates. Most of the original deciduous trees have long gone, but many yews have survived. Being vulnerable to wind-blow on the steep slopes, they have been pruned where necessary. The woodland is being replanted and the bank above the path is being filled with hollies and thorns to improve security and separate the garden from the now busy and noisy Ralph Allen Drive.

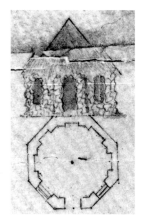

The octagonal thatched house on Thorpe and Overton's *Survey* of c.1762. Only the foundations remain

The Rock Gate in the 1750s; sketch by Thomas Robins. The stone was a pitted limestone often used in British grottoes